Just This

Just This

New and Selected Poems

John Brehm

Wisdom

Wisdom Publications
132 Perry Street
New York, NY 10014 USA
wisdom.org

Library of Congress Cataloging-in-Publication Data
Names: Brehm, John, 1955– author
Title: Just this: new & selected poems / John Brehm.
Other titles: Just this (Compilation)
Description: New York, NY: Wisdom, 2026.
Identifiers: LCCN 2025045316 (print) | LCCN 2025045317 (ebook) |
    ISBN 9798890700520 paperback acid-free paper |
    ISBN 9798890700582 ebook
Subjects: LCGFT: Poetry
Classification: LCC PS3602.R444 J87 2026 (print) |
    LCC PS3602.R444 (ebook)
LC record available at https://lccn.loc.gov/2025045316
LC ebook record available at https://lccn.loc.gov/2025045317

ISBN 979-8-89070-052-0   ebook ISBN 979-8-89070-058-2

30 29 28 27 26   5 4 3 2 1

Cover design by Marc Whitaker. Interior design by Tim Holtz. Set in
Adobe Caslon Pro 10/14.

Publisher's edition of select poems from *Sea of Faith*, *Help Is on the Way*, and
No Day at the Beach by John Brehm is published by arrangement with the
University of Wisconsin Press. © by John Brehm. All rights reserved.

Printed on acid-free paper that meets the guidelines for permanence and
durability of the Production Guidelines for Book Longevity of the Council
on Library Resources.

Printed in the United States of America.

MIX
Paper | Supporting
responsible forestry
FSC® C005010

Please visit fscus.org.

Do you want to know what's in my heart?
From the beginning of time: just this! just this!

—Ryokan

Contents

FROM *SEA OF FAITH* (2004)

FROM *HELP IS ON THE WAY* (2012)

FROM *NO DAY AT THE BEACH* (2020)

FROM *DHARMA TALK* (2023)

for Andrea Hollander

New Poems

I

Oncology Waiting Room

Into a vase of wilted purple roses
the receptionist drops
an aspirin.

Visitation with the Radiologist

"It's not a good disease to have," my doctor says.
I admire his grim honesty, I admire it
greatly. "Indolent, but it usually does progress."
Which sounds about right for me.
Two years of misdiagnosed torment
and now this. I ask him about suicide.
He nods. "It happens," he says.
When I tell him I've seriously considered it,
he says my disease would qualify me
for Death with Dignity, because
it's incurable, though I might not meet
the six-months-to-live criteria,
just the unendurable pain part. Which will
come back after I've exhausted all the treatments.
"But they might make an exception
if it's a choice between bending the rules
and blowing your brains out."
This is my doctor, telling the truth, filters off.
I slide down into it as into a warm bath.
I want to stay here forever, ask him every question.
Maybe death is speaking through him.
What's it like on the other side? I want to ask.
Once you're dead, do you stop worrying
about what people think of you?

Are you allowed to intervene in the affairs
of the living, offer invisible advice now and then,
a nudge on the arm? How shall I live
with the time I have left is the real question.
I don't ask it but let it blossom
into the room. This, this conversation,
this way of speaking, turns me
toward an answer.

Side Effects

Side effects may include brain fog, fatigue,
an overall "blah" feeling. You may
experience blurred vision.
The world may begin to look
sepia-toned.

Childhood memories of carefree joy
may become inaccessible.

Future happiness may appear
to disappear.

The present may seem drained
of color, of texture,
of life itself.

Contact your doctor right away if you notice
a subtle increase in your receptivity
to gravity, or if it seems you are
walking underwater,
or over-vivifying your visions
of personal and collective catastrophe,
or are sleepless for more
than six months,

or feel you have entered
what Gabriel García Márquez called
the endless Sunday afternoons of death.

But don't despair. Don't. Something clean and clear
awaits you on the other side of all this.

The Importance of Sleep

Why does every book about sleep begin by listing
all the terrible consequences of *not* sleeping?
Increased risk of heart disease, kidney disease,
high blood pressure, diabetes, obesity, stroke,
depression, dementia: jet fuel for the 3 a.m.
ruminations. And if it's so important, why
did God make good sleep almost impossible
to get? God, the irritable, eternal insomniac.
The dreamer-up of fantastic human torments,
the vast array of diseases and afflictions
the human body is heir to, dazzling in their
infinite variety and weirdness. For example,
a friend of mine has eczema of the inner ear.
His partner has two kinds of cancer, prostate
and bladder. Another friend has face blindness.
She can't recognize the faces even of her own
husband or stepchildren. Another lives in a tent
because almost everything—fumes, noise,
mold, other people—poisons him. And then
there's my nephew who died of porphyria,
a rare blood disorder that causes extreme
sensitivity to sunlight and is thought to be
the origin of the vampire myth. WTF, God?
Seriously, you're like a child torturing insects.

How can anybody sleep knowing you're up there
looking down on us, steeped in your power,
reaching for your magnifying glass?

Meditation

The tingling in my feet
when I let my
attention fall to them—
what is that?

A distant call from
deep in the earth itself?

A reminder
of where I'm from
and where I'm headed?

The pull of gravity, as
a form of love?

Or "gravity, the silent killer,"
as someone once said,
someone likely
now dead.

What We Want on Our Headstones

For my friend it's: WHAT THE FUCK WAS *THAT*
    ABOUT?
or just WHAT THE FUCK? I'm leaning toward
SERIOUSLY? or WAS ALL THAT REALLY NECESSARY?

I like to think our spirits would be amused
to look down and see the reactions of people
solemnly on their way to pay respects to loved ones.

A little smile, some quiet laughter, or better still
an irrepressible guffaw in the graveyard
would please us for all eternity.

On Pain and Suffering

Pain is a great teacher, people often say.
But is it, really? It's true I've learned new ways
of wincing, of swearing, of limping.
Of shouting in my sleep, waking and
worrying my wife, who is herself
a great teacher, and a kind one.
Why can't we exalt kindness,
not just as a form of benevolence
but a source of wisdom? I've learned
more from the kindness of others than from
pain and suffering, which at their worst
leave me clenched and self-obsessed,
narrowing the field of my concern
to making the pain stop, full stop.
Nothing else matters, not even the ordeals
of my dearest friends, I'm embarrassed
to admit. Where's the great lesson in that?

"Life, it seems, explains nothing about itself,"
wrote James Schuyler, a poet who suffered
psychotic breaks, and once covered
his naked body with dollar bills, insisting
he was Jesus Christ, and scaring the crap
out of a young Ron Padgett, with whom

he was staying. Was he a better man, or stronger,
for having lived through such horror?
I doubt he would have thought so.
I imagine it diminished him, the humiliation,
the madness and chaos, all meaningless.
Still, he kept it going—the poems, his life.

And so I bow to you, James Schuyler,
and if I learn from anyone, I learn from you,
not from your suffering but from all
you were able to see and name and feel,
the barn owl "circling the field on owl-silent wings,"
the bluet that broke you up, "tiny spring flower
late, late in dour October," in those moments
when pain set you free.

Primal Knowledge

Now I waddle around like a wounded duck
because of the pain in my hips, back, and feet,
saying *fuck, fuck, fuck* under my breath.

The other day I tripped going up the stairs
and fell forward and landed hard.
Now I know that falling flat on your face

is more than a metaphor. I have a black eye
and a cut above my right eyebrow to prove it.
I'm wondering if I should meet my friend Justin

at a café or invite him here so I won't
have to attempt my trippy walking in public.
You hardly ever see limping people

out and about. I look for them, my brethren,
and they do not appear, maybe because
of the primal knowledge that the weakest

in the herd will be watched and chased
and set upon by predators. But I haven't
left the house in four days and I'm not

going stir crazy so much as worrying
that this will become my shrunken life,
my captivity: sitting around, watching TV,

gazing out the window, remembering long
hikes in the mountains, in the old growth
above the river, and nodding off from time

to time as my mother often did when she
was about fifteen years older than I am now.
She had her own crushing back pain,

and did I ever try to imagine what that
was like for her? I don't think so.
Now I know for sure.

Poem About Nothing

The only thing happening
this early hour is nothing:

people sleeping, the weight
of their unconsciousness

darkening the air, loading
the clouds with dreamstuff;

a crow, barely visible, like
a piece of the night itself

broken off, given wings
and a raw voice, quiet now,

saying nothing, an emissary
of silence; a stack of books

on the side of my desk, one
thin volume standing tentlike

on top of the others,
a thing one is not supposed

to do with books, according
to my father-in-law, asleep

down the hall. All those poems,
alive beneath their covers,

little fires of consciousness
still burning, waiting

for a mind to fan the flames.
Long after / the call to prayer /

the bell rope swaying.
Warmth and light are what

I want from poems, quiet
from morning, sound advice

from a father-in-law, even if
I don't follow it.

To-Do List

Start a to-do list. Consult it every day,
first thing in the morning. Ditto
the calendar. No more
double booking! Get new glasses.
Tidy up closets and desk drawers.
Entropy is real, apparently.
Break down the boxes in the basement
and take to the recycling bin.
Call the handyman.
Answer emails from Timothy,
Marc, Heather, and someone else.
Pick more blueberries before the jays
remember where they are.
Water the plants, extra for the begonias.
Finish the book on climate change
by the Dalai Lama and Greta Thunberg.
Pray for inspiration, for guidance,
for the flourishing and good fortune
of my friends, for the wars to end,
for the collective awakening
my teacher says is "a done deal."
Get more sleep. Be more optimistic.
Reread Schuyler and Bishop. Choose one

or both, as Schuyler liked to say.
Clean the bird bath.
Have faith.

What He Looks Like

Holding a steel rake
high above his head,
stalking small fish
that nipped his ankles,
the boy says, *I must
look like the grim reaper.*
His sister, lazing on
the beach, peering over
her sunglasses, replies:
You look like an idiot.

Update

I'm like a dead tree still standing.
My shoots won't shoot,
my buds are duds,
my bark's got no bite,
my lumber's no longer limber,
and all my leaves have left.
Birds fly right by me,
they do not come to rest
or nest or sing in my branches.
The acrobatic squirrels
no longer cavort, nor chase
and chatter. I'm told
the gray ones are invasive.
The chestnut ones I loved
are gone.

Prayer

Love is real, fear an illusion—
that's what the mushrooms
taught me that day thirty

years ago in Prospect Park,
my eyes so clear I could see
a bird's eye a hundred feet away

and could tell it was seeing me,
wanted me to *know* it was
seeing me. I saw a Hasidic man

pacing back and forth reading
a sacred text. I saw a witch-like
woman in a long black coat bent

over the ground with an eye-dropper
squeezing something into the earth.
I'm not sure either of them

was really there. Now, my mind
made desolate by illness
and the drugs I take to treat it,

I long for that magic, the certainty
I felt then that the universe
is a friendly place, love

the only reality, fear just a habit
we inherited, a dream we can't
wake up from. Now I long

to see and say something
beautiful, something that would
redeem this suffering, sanctify it,

or at least make it more bearable.
If that is not too much to ask.

Reprieve

Please don't knock down all the leaves, rain.
Not just as they've turned to deepest reds
and softest yellows, parchment paper
the thin autumnal light shines clear through.
Please let them last a little longer, wind.
I know that clinging is wrong, in people
as in leaves, but please grant a temporary
exception in this one instance
to the law of impermanence.
Every year we get a day like this
in early November, reckless weather
abolishing the show at its peak, the glorious
painterly trees and bushes I take photos of
to identify so that they might be added
to our garden, so desirous am I
not merely to see but to possess this beauty.
It's not that I don't love the starkness
of empty branches, trees fiercely standing
and withstanding winter's coldest cold.
I do. But please let this burst of color keep on
for now, for a while longer. I'm not
quite ready for the darkness
that comes after.

II

now that I'm old and sick
everyone saying
    how good I look

gift of aging—
the haiku I read last week
new again!

I remember
to use my forgetfulness
as an excuse

just before dawn
my tinnitus takes over
where the crickets leave off

newspaper ad:
"Are you hard of hearing?"
     shouldn't it be in all caps?

bonsai shop . . .
what shape
would I take?

sunlit path
first the shadow falls
then the leaf

tip of the tongue
I can almost taste
the wayward word

looking up
from looking something up—
    the whole world still there

they take turns
raindrops
        falling from the eaves

summer storm
the same thunder
I heard as a child

she leans a little
to hold the umbrella
over her small white dog

rehearsing the argument . . .
fallen leaves
on the path

no self—
a water strider shatters
my reflection on the pond

so thin!
the cat's ear
   backlit by morning sun

writer's block—
the cat rests her chin
on my right hand

long-winded
and short-sighted
the poet goes on and on

perfect typo
the *wandering* now *wondering*
monks

I forgive myself
for failing
to forgive myself

tomorrow
I'm going to start
living in the present

burst of wildflowers—
　　laughter
　　　　in the neighbor's yard

reading to just four people—
one smile
        makes the empty chairs disappear

after the updates
on our afflictions
        we bring out the poems

FROM *Sea of Faith* (2004)

Layabout

Do nothing and everything will be done,
that's what Lao Tzu said, who wandered
around in tattered robes 2,500 years ago

and now his book practically grows on trees
it's so popular and if he were alive
today hordes of seekers would

rush up to him like waves lapping
at the shores of his wisdom.
That's the way it is, I guess: humbling.

But if I could just unclench my fists,
empty out my eyes, turn my mind into
a prayer flag for the wind to play with,

we could be brothers, him the older one
who's seen and not done it all and me
still unlearning, both of us slung low

in our hammocks, our hats tipped
forwards, hands folded neatly,
like bamboo huts above our hearts.

If Feeling Isn't in It

you can take it away, as far as I'm concerned—
I'd rather spend the afternoon with a nice dog.
I'm not kidding. Dogs have what a lot of poems
lack: excitements and responses, a sense of play,
the ability to impart warmth, elation . . .
                                              —Howard Moss

Dogs will also lick your face if you let them.
Their bodies will shiver with happiness.
A simple walk in the park is just about
the height of contentment for them, followed
by a bowl of food, a bowl of water,
a place to curl up and sleep. Someone
to scratch them where they can't reach
and smooth their foreheads and talk to them.
Dogs also have a natural dislike of mailmen
and other bringers of bad news and will
bite them on your behalf. Dogs can smell
fear and also love with perfect accuracy.
There is no use pretending with them.
Nor do they pretend. If a dog is happy
or sad or nervous or bored or ashamed
or sunk in contemplation, everybody knows it.
They make no secret of themselves.

You can even tell what they're dreaming about
by the way their legs jerk and try to run
on the slippery ground of sleep.
Nor are they given to pretentious self-importance.
They don't try to impress you with how serious
or sensitive they are. They just feel everything
full blast. Everything is off the charts
with them. More than once I've seen a dog
waiting for its owner outside a café
practically *implode* with worry. "Oh, God,
what if she doesn't come back this time?
What will I do? Who will take care of me?
I loved her so much and now she's gone
and I'm tied to a post surrounded by people
who don't look or smell or sound like her at all."
And when she does come, what a flurry
of commotion, what a chorus of yelping
and cooing and leaps straight up into the air!
It's almost unbearable, this sudden
fullness after such total loss, to see
the world made whole again by a hand
on the shoulder and a voice like no other.

At Coney Island

Strange tubas in my ears and the fat
yellow light lolling across
the boardwalk doesn't
exactly help and of course
elephants lumbering
through one's thoughts
remembering where they
must go to die is not
the pleasantest of situations
either and the ocean
what can you say about it?
It hardly knows itself
but there it is the one
and the many waves all doing
whatever waves do, lapping
doggedly at the shore,
making a splash, lending
themselves unwisely
to human metaphor,
the whole earth meanwhile
spinning through space
like a basketball on the tip
of an idle god's finger.
People stroll by eating

hot dogs, heroes, corn-
on-the-cob, wildly purple
bursts of cotton candy
and other members
of the colorful, hard-
to-believe food groups.
Well, some of us do a pretty
decent job of amusing ourselves
here where the land
meets the sea and music
empties the air
of silence. This is what
we crawled up out of
four hundred million years ago.
And this is what
we've become now that
we've dried ourselves off.
Creatures so fearful
of death we'll actually
get on a rollercoaster
just to calm ourselves down.
This is the much needed
transfusion of the outer
to the inner world.
Elephants, tubas, fat light
falling across the bathers
asleep on the shore

of the Atlantic Ocean.
Their children splashing
each other in the freezing water.

When My Car Broke Down

I was somewhere in Utah or Wyoming,
somewhere in the high inhuman deserts,
in the thin blue flame of wavering air,
bluffs of red earth scorched and

stratified on the horizon. I had stopped
to admire the desolation, to smoke
a cigarette and consider that ten thousand
years ago this was all under water,

that strange fish would have swum
through the space my eyes now occupied;
before that ice, and before that
something else again, unimaginably alien.

Chögyam Trungpa says first thought best thought,
but my first thought when I saw the steam
billowing up from under my car was:
if I just keep driving, maybe it will go away.

After all, I was moving three thousand miles
not to "escape" my problems but to put
a nice distance between them and me.
A problem has to be fierce to travel that far.

My second thought was to stare at the engine
for a while. I leaned over and looked
down into it as into the bowels of a ship
or the cranium of some fantastic beast.

And recalled how my father tried to teach me
about cars. Mostly he had me hold
the light for hours and mostly I studied
the back of his head, turning over the words

he said and knowing even then I'd never
understand. The blood would drain
from my arm and I'd prop it up
with my one free hand to keep from

caving in or betraying my halfheartedness.
Even then I was hopelessly afflicted
with the disease of the Wandering Mind.
Even then I was dreaming myself

across magical landscapes, just like this,
and learning all he had to teach me
about standing rooted to one spot,
wishing I were somewhere else.

My Emotions Are Like Fish

Mostly they live in the dark
underwater weed-slithering
currents and worry about

being swallowed up by their
more furious brethren.
Some of them have eyes

perched atop long thin stems
like flowers. And some
have forty or fifty arms

pocked with suction cups
to help them stick to things
and will squirt black

clouds of ink to keep
themselves concealed. Others
resemble subtropical

dottybacks or scaleless deepsea
gulper eels, with their
velvety bodies, zipper teeth,

and whip-like tails. The fearsome
dragonfish—likewise the
viperfish, hatchetfish,

and bristlemouth—all find their
corollaries in the Red Sea
of my heart. Even

the phantom glass catfish,
entirely translucent except
for its intestines,

is no stranger to my feelings.
The unforthcoming among them
behave just like shovelnose

stingrays who flop right down
in the bottom-ooze and flick
the muck up over them.

But some of them, when they
swim too near the surface,
find themselves suddenly

exalted, lifted and flying
through the air, wind-filled,
sunlight-sharpened sky

expanding around them, high
above their proper element—
birdclaws sunk into their backs.

Love Stories

In such ecstasy suffering begins,
or so I tell myself, passing
the pairs of lovers splayed
like Christs along the lawn

behind the library, in whose
books no further shall they
read today. They read each
other's eyes instead and find

a story there at once fantastic
and familiar, a story they
composed themselves, years ago,
and only half-remember now.

How it ends is what they can't
recall, how their eyes,
dimly lit in love's dilation,
will narrow and harden and

turn away. On the gravel path
that borders the park, I place
myself like an asterisk
in the margin to mark a curious

passage. I could certainly provide
a gloss on what they're going
through, but it would be just
another story, the one I tell

myself about the one they
tell themselves about each other.

Postcard from the Heartbreak Hotel

Wish you were here instead of me.
It has a fantastic view
of the vast unconscious ocean,
into which a few of the guests
will no doubt fling themselves
before their stay is through.
The rooms are so spacious
and so clean you'd think
you were the first person
ever to not sleep here.
The beds of course are huge,
an abyss of white sheets around you
which you may fill with your
imagination whatever way you wish.
The staff—courteous, attentive,
remorseless—anticipates your
every need and frustrates them all.
The food, as you may guess,
is a tasteless affair, some grey
monotonous gruel we make up
poems about. "Cruel," "fool,"
"wool," (as in over your eyes)
and "autopsy" seem to be
the favorite rhyme words.

And lately the guests have
devised a new game: who
can stare out the window
longest without seeing anything.
We've been told the mountains
before us are astonishing.
But we've made them disappear.
Reduced them to a blank
gray screen on which
to play out the home movies
of our despair again and again.
And when the sun sets and
darkness reaches out its arms
around the world like a man
gathering his winnings off a table,
the tree outside my window
becomes your back
receding down the hall.
All night the neon sign
glows in self-conscious irony.
Yes, there is a vacancy.

Sea of Faith

Once when I was teaching "Dover Beach"
to a class of freshmen, a young woman
raised her hand and said, "I'm confused
about this 'Sea of Faith.'" "Well," I said,
"let's talk about it. We probably need
to talk a bit about figurative language.
What confuses you about it?"
"I mean, is it a real sea?" she asked.
"You mean, is it a real body of water
that you could point to on a map
or visit on a vacation?"
"Yes," she said. "Is it a *real* sea?"
Oh Christ, I thought, is this where we are?
Next year I'll be teaching them the alphabet
and how to sound words out.
I'll have to teach them geography, apparently,
before we can move on to poetry.
I'll have to teach them history, too—
a few weeks on the Dark Ages might be instructive.
"Yes," I wanted to say, "it is.
It is a real sea. In fact it flows
right into the Sea of Ignorance
IN WHICH YOU ARE DROWNING.

Let me throw you a Rope of Salvation
before the Sharks of Desire gobble you up.
Let me hoist you back up onto this Ship of Fools
so that we might continue our search
for the Fountain of Youth. Here, take a drink
of this. It's fresh from the River of Forgetfulness."
But of course I didn't say any of that.
I tried to explain in such a way
as to protect her from humillation,
tried to explain that poets
often speak of things that don't exist.
It was only much later that I wished
I could have answered differently,
only after I'd betrayed myself
and been betrayed that I wished
it was true, wished there really was a Sea of Faith
that you could wade out into,
dive under its blue and magic waters,
hold your breath, swim like a fish
down to the bottom, and then emerge again
able to believe in everything, faithful
and unafraid to ask even the simplest of questions,
happy to have them simply answered.

The Poems I Have Not Written

I'm so wildly unprolific, the poems
I have not written would reach
from here to the California coast
if you laid them end to end.

And if you stacked them up,
the poems I have not written
would sway like a silent
Tower of Babel, saying nothing

and everything in a thousand
different tongues. So moving, so
filled with and emptied of suffering,
so steeped in the music of a voice

speechless before the truth,
the poems I have not written
would break the hearts of every
woman who's ever left me,

make them eye their husbands
with a sharp contempt and hate
themselves for turning their backs
on the very source of beauty.

The poems I have not written
would compel all other poets
to ask of God: "*Why* do you
let me live? I am worthless.

Please strike me dead at once,
destroy my works and cleanse
the earth of all my ghastly
imperfections." Trees would

bow their heads before the poems
I have not written. "Take me,"
they would say, "and turn me
into your pages so that I

might live forever as the ground
from which your words arise."
The wind itself, about which
I might have written so eloquently,

praising its slick and intersecting
rivers of air, its stately calms
and furious interrogations,
its flutelike lingerings and passionate

reproofs, would divert its course
to sweep down and then pass over
the poems I have not written,
and the life I have not lived, the life

I've failed even to imagine,
which they so perfectly describe.

Landscape Survey

And what about this boulder,
knocked off the mountaintop and
tumbled down a thousand years ago

to lodge against the streambank,
does it waste itself with worry
about how things are going

to turn out? Does the current
slicing around it stop itself mid-
stream because it can't get past

all it's left behind back at
the source or up in the clouds
where its waters first fell

to earth? And these trees,
would they double over and
clutch themselves or lash out

furiously if they were to discover
what the other trees really
thought of them? Would the wind

reascend into the sky forever,
like an in-drawn breath,
if it knew it was fated simply

to sweep the earth of windlessness,
to touch everything and keep
nothing and be beheld by no one?

Sound Check, Lower Manhattan

Just a jumble of songs and jackhammers and
roaring garbage trucks, people talking
or shouting, a bitterly thin old man lying
L-shaped against a building in SoHo saying
"What am I gonna do?" over and over,
swept under in the city's onrushing
waves of noise, its piercing sirens
and superfluous car alarms
and subways gurgling underground,
the low invisible hum of the buildings
themselves, as if breathing, their great
tired bodies standing all these years
wishing to lie down and rest,
and the quiet intensity of people
saying nothing, turning in on themselves,
the soft click of their eyes in passing,
the undercurrent of their thought
moving like a wind through
the sidewalks thronging with life
and the sound of life and the silence
that is death waiting behind it all saying have
your noise yes make as much as you can,
and now the bright yellow brass
of car horns clashing in the air

above Broadway, the street itself
impatient, running like a black stream
down to the harbor, into the East River,
buses heaving and lurching like
elephants dragged from another world
and made to work here where no
one can sit still, where music spills
from opening doors and floats
like trash into the sky, where a man
can ask his one question forever
and never hear an answer.

The Blasted Tree

Of all of them along the path
that curved for twenty miles
through thickest forest, it was
the blasted tree I loved best.
Among thousands of firs
risen beyond the eye's reach,
among colossal cedars
with their bark soft
as humid earth, among
groves of slender birches that
filtered winds cast across
these hills from Asia,
among even the hemlocks, gripped
in rocky ground and holding
two hundred years of darkness
in each leaf, among all these
it was the blasted oak
I loved best. Just as the path
turns and ascends, it stands
in a little clearing, like
a signpost to the walker
who would go on farther, as if
to say there is some price
to be paid, or only

the stricken may enter here.
Perhaps because it stood alone
the lightning bolt found its way to it,
the branch that would have arched
above and shaded the meadow
torn off in a brilliant flash
of the sky's violence, ripped cleanly
from the trunk, though you can
still see the black scorched
teeth of the wood where
it broke and let
the limb fall to earth.
It must have been a ghastly
sound and a sight heart-
breaking to behold, the perfect
symmetry and elegance gone
in an instant. And now
a piece of sky no one would
ever have seen from here
comes clearly into view,
empty and blue and cleaner
than before because of
the branch's vivid absence.
I loved the damaged grandeur
of that tree, how it bore
its loss with such composure
and kept on growing,

lopsided, irreparable, beautiful,
the catastrophe of its history
written on its body.
And though I am not one
who's been appointed to say
what trees may mean,
it was no mystery why it could hold
me so still, compel my eye
to such study, whenever
I passed that way.

The Fence

Thirty years ago and still I cannot get beyond it,
that day my father and my uncle led me
up the mountainside, high in the Sierra Nevada,
to where the water slid down from snowmelt
gathering speed and depth and force to shape
itself into the narrow rock-bed that fell
in a brilliant curl half a mile above the house.
So clear my uncle said he ran a pipe straight
down to the kitchen, so clear he said you could
piss in it and twenty yards downstream drink it
again, purified, better than any city water ever was.
When we got there, out of breath, I dipped
my hand and let it flutter against the current
and fall away, then cupped it and brought
the water, a colder condensation of the cold
mountain air, to my lips and drank. I seemed
to breathe it into my veins like an exaltation.
I turned and looked down through the pine trees,
their needles bright and precise, sharpened,
like nerves, oscillating in the sheer winds
that blew at those heights, and then I took
two steps and began to run, slowly at first
to keep my balance between the rocks and trees
and loose dirt that scratched and slipped beneath me.

And then I let myself lean forward, headlong
into the downward pull, found an open pathway
and gave into it, running hard and then harder
just to keep up with myself, just to keep
myself upright, sucked into that dizzying
acceleration, my legs pounding the earth, my arms
flipping up and down like pistons, the air
tearing through me until I was all speed
and the pure exhilaration of a body flying
full-tilt down a mountainside, the mind
shifting into muscle and joint and bone, shedding
consciousness like a dead skin to slip out
wholly into that fluid animal motion.
And then, just as the trees flicked past me
and I could not see, just as the wind
shook inside my head so I could not hear
my father's voice lost in the air above me,
just as I was about to burst beyond myself,
I stopped, slammed into myself, came up dead still,
my heart suspended somewhere in the back of my neck,
and stood there, in an electric calm, and looked
down to see, two inches from my belly,
a barbed-wire fence—three strands, taut,
glittering exactly in the sunlight before me.
I had not seen it, had not known it was there,
could not have stopped had I seen or known.
And I felt how clearly it should have cut me,

or caught me, or torn me through to the other side,
how still I stood there, studying that limit,
suddenly split, some other part of me gone through,
gone past it further down the mountainside
to wait for me, or to burn itself out as it might
reach again the falling stream and dissolve cleanly
within the waterfall, or to go on running still,
set loose, it now occurs to me, on a course
around the earth, perfectly timed to hit me
full force in the back some day years and years
from now, as I stand absently looking on, asking
over and over how it possibly could have happened.

Supplication at the River

And then I would turn away
and into something other,
as if the way the water moves,
confluence of sources, metaphor
for everything, but essential and itself,
would be my way of moving.

As if there really were some
possibilities, some place to go,
not just this repetition of first losses.
As if the self could be a departure,
even if only through a fresh grief,
that would be a returning and a beginning.

As if the water that I am
might find a better form,
rise above, in a body composed
of something other than lust and sorrow,
or simply slip down into this water,
which atones, and forgets, and need not speak.

Passage

In all the woods that day I was
the only living thing
fretful, exhausted, or unsure.
Giant fir and spruce and cedar trees
that had stood their ground
three hundred years
stretched in sunlight calmly
unimpressed by whatever
it was that held me
hunched and tense above the stream,
biting my nails, calculating all
my impossibilities.
Nor did the water pause
to reflect or enter into
my considerations.
It found its way
over and around a crowd
of rocks in easy flourishes,
in laughing evasions and
shifts in direction.
Nothing could slow it down for long.

It even made a little song
out of all the things
that got in its way,
a music against the hard edges
of whatever might interrupt its going.

The Inner Life

I'm tired of the inner life
with all its wrangling voices
and combustible insights.
Tired of its shadowy caves
that seem to say: "You might
want to spend a few years
looking around in here."
Tired of being drenched in
that darkness that won't
wash off and drives the sun,
like a smiling friend, away.
Tired of discovering who I am
from one day to the next.
The Origin and History of My
Neuroses, Vols. I–XXVII,
no longer tempts me to lift
its weighty covers, turn the pages
that creak like floorboards,
and study again the famous
battles, failed negotiations,
broken treaties, and felled
combatants still littering the field.

"Know thyself." Sure, of course,
you must. But afterwards
the project is to make yourself
a stranger to yourself once more.

Nine-to-Five

Take two sabbaticals and call me
in the morning that's what
he said but all I want

is to live alone on an island
unmetaphorically poised
above a sea flippant

with dolphins far from all
these assertive people
forever trying to

remake the world in their own
circus-mirror self-image.
I want the world to

remake me in *its* image teach me
how to live like a weed
or a pile of sand or

a cloud shredded over and
over again by the wind
or the wind itself

locked into the sky and out
of everything else or like
one transparent

wave far offshore through
which the playful and
the deadly slip.

Mistakes of One Kind or Another

A friend of mine once had a student
who wrote: "In the great body
of English literature, John Milton
stands out as a vital organ."

What do you say to that? At least
he didn't leave the modifier dangling.
And in a class of mine on racism,
no fewer than four students wrote

essays discussing the plight of the
"escapegoat." I remember blinking,
thinking it must be a typo.
But, no, the word appeared again

and again until at last I saw that
solemn beast take shape to stand
forlorn in a field beyond
a barbed-wire fence, exhausted,

bewildered, in leg-irons and prison stripes,
looking back over his shoulder
at the world that needed him so badly,
for which he bore so many names,

and wondering where he might go
to be free of such blame, such dark
projections of the guilt of others,
such innocent misunderstandings.

Sotto Voce

To strip away this incessant chatter,
yes, but what lies underneath it?

Death, of course, or our fear of death.
Which is why we talk so much,

bury our heads in books, turn forests
into pages and pages into mirrors

in which we see ourselves appear
and disappear. When I look up

from the book I've been reading
about the Jews in Nazi Germany

and the silence that closed their
mouths forever, I see a girl outside

the café smiling in at her father
who smiles back but cannot hear her.

She makes all kinds of gestures
with her hands, mimes herself

inside an invisible box and breaks
down laughing. Then she gathers

her breath and blows it against
the window. It is not snowing

outside, the leaves have hardly begun
to turn, the season is merely poised

for the long descent, but still
the glass steams up. And in this

little cloud of warmth that rises
from deep inside her body, she

writes a single joyful word, which
vanishes almost before she finishes.

Autumn

It is to the small satisfactions
we must return, for surely
the great ones fail us.
The unexpected face, the way
evening's slow descent, when
everything is poised for her
arrival, astonishes the day.
And then the steady, familiar
things, houses and trees, suddenly
precise, alive and themselves.
These will do for us now,
now that we have given up on
matters of brooding consequence,
now that such a leisure
of wind, studying the leaves
more closely, lifts them up,
bright in the pure, black air.

FROM *Help Is on the Way*
(2012)

Pompeii

Standing on the subway, exhausted, dispirited,
glancing over the exhausted, dispirited faces
of my fellow passengers, I read posters
for a new movie about Pompeii.
"How can you breathe when the air is on fire?"
"How can you escape a boiling mudslide?"
"How can you outrun an eruption
faster than this train?" they ask.
Obviously the ad writer has never been
on *this* train, because this is a Q train,
and anybody who can't outrun a Q train
must be on death's doorstep anyway
and will soon be overtaken by time itself,
if not a boiling mudslide, though sometimes
that's what time feels like, thick
and burning, pushing you on and pulling
you back. And now we rise creaking
over the Manhattan Bridge, where
one can see through scratchy windows
the city skyline and the buildings that are
not there, where thousands tried
to breathe air on fire and failed,
tried to flee an avalanche of concrete
and falling bodies and failed.

If only they'd been asked to outrun something
as slow as this slow train that takes us home—
how easily they might have done it.
But that is not what they were asked to do.

Valid Photo Identification Required

I don't understand myself, nor do I know myself, nor
can I explain or prove who I am to anyone else.
All I know is that I'm a man who let his out-
of-state driver's license expire and who
does not have his original Social Security Card,
(issued at birth?) or a copy of said document,
to obtain which one must have an unexpired
driver's license, which requires, of course, a valid
Social Security Card. I needed something to get me
on a plane at LaGuardia. I did have a birth certificate,
and when I slid it tentatively under the bullet-proof
Plexiglas window at the Brooklyn Social Security Office
and said, "What about this?" to the unexpectedly
sympathetic and ontologically sophisticated young
Asian-American man scanning my application
for a replacement card, he looked at me and said,
"This doesn't help. This just proves you were born.
We need proof of your *continued* existence."
I threw up my hands and looked down at my body,
as if to say, Well, I'm standing here, aren't I?
I admit I have not done much with this life.
I have failed at love, let down my friends,
ignored my best instincts and given my worst ones
free play, but for better or worse I *have* continued

to exist. Because if I *hadn't* continued to exist,
I wouldn't be contemplating all the joys and deep
satisfactions of nonexistence, as I am right now.
I don't imagine the dead are required to show papers
at every river crossing, or that only those with valid
photo ID are allowed into the caldron,
or harpsichord concert, as the case may be. Often I wake
at 3 a.m., I wanted to tell him, with the night terrors,
scrambled fears of death, which would be one
of the privileges conferred exclusively upon the living,
and often I wish I could forget myself completely,
forget the fragile, worried, rabbit-hearted self
that seems to run my life, forget the whole
nightmarish mess—I wouldn't have that
feeling if I hadn't continued to exist, would I?
It's true, I wanted to confess, I have no children
to mirror me into the future, and mostly I only
half-inhabit the poems I've written, a ghostly
uneasy absence floating just below the lines.
In fact, from the Buddhist perspective
I don't exist, but neither do you, nor any of this.
A luminous emptiness is all there is.
Instead I tell him I just want to visit my parents,
for Christmas, in Nebraska, for Christ's sake.
Which was no help.

Of Love and Life Insurance: An Argument

"I need to accept you as you are," she said,
"so you need to become the kind
of person I can accept." I was
becoming bewildered, but I don't
think that's what she meant.
"Life insurance," she said. "You
don't have any life insurance."
"But we've only known each other
three months. Aren't we jumping ahead?"
"Look," she said, "I don't want
to have to take my child and move
back to Chicago and live with my mother.
I don't want to have to take my child
to a public clinic. And I don't want
to have to ride you and nag you and ask you
a hundred times about all this stuff."
And then my heart fell from the sky
like a shot bird. "Is *that* how you
imagine a life with me?"
I guess being an unsuccessful poet
isn't as attractive as it used to be.
But where's the risky spirit,
the headlong leap into the vast
unknown of love, where anything

and everything might happen? Where's
the wish to be surrounded by poems,
the great sustaining luxuries and dangers
of poems, or to make one's life itself
a poem, unpredictable, meaning
many things, a door into the other world
through which even a child might walk?
Words have such power, I wanted to tell her.
You never know what may come of them.
Or who will be the beneficiary.

Getting Where We're Going

Surfeit of distance and the wracked mind waiting,
nipping at itself, snarling inwardly at strangers.
If I had a car in this town I'd
rig it up with a rear bumper horn,
something to blast back at the jackasses
who honk the second the light turns green.
If you could gather up all the hornhonks
of just one day in New York City,
tie them together in a big brassy knot
high above the city and honk
them all at once, it would shiver
the skyscrapers to nothingness, as if
they were made of sand, and usher
in the Second Coming. Christ would descend
from the sky wincing with his fingers
in his ears and judge us all insane.
Who'd want people like us up there,
yelling at each other, trashing the cloudy,
angelic streets with our candy wrappers
and newspapers and coffee cups?
Besides, we'd still be waiting for
the next thing to happen in Heaven,
the next violin concerto or cotton-candy
festival or breathtaking vista to open

beneath our feet, and thinking this place
isn't quite what it's cracked up to be,
and why in hell does everybody
want to get here? We'd still be
waiting for someone else to come
and make us happy, staring through
whatever's in front of us, cursing the light
that never seems to change.

Change in Service

"Attention passengers, there is no uptown
local service on the 1 train at this time.
Repeat, there is no uptown
local service on the 1 train at this time.
For uptown local service, transfer
at 14th Street across the platform
to the downtown number 2 train.
Take the downtown number 2 train
to Chambers Street. At Chambers Street,
transfer to shuttle bus service
for South Street Ferry. At South
Street Ferry, take a Circle Line
Sightseeing Cruise Ship up
the East River to the 59th Street Bridge.
At the 59th Street Bridge, fling
yourself overboard and swim
to Roosevelt Island.
From Roosevelt Island, take
the Tramway back to Manhattan.
Exit the Tramway
and take a cab to the FDR
Expressway. Proceed north
on the FDR Expressway
to the George Washington Bridge.

Cross the George Washington Bridge
and take the Palisades Parkway
north to Piermont. At Piermont,
rent a kayak and paddle down
the Hudson River to 96th and Riverside.
From 96th and Riverside
walk east to Central Park West,
turn right on Central Park West
and proceed south to Columbus Circle.
At Columbus Circle take a rickshaw
to 42nd Street Times Square.
At 42nd Street Times Square, ride the escalator
down past the Fellini-esque organist
with the swiveling, trumpet-
playing monkey dolls
and board the uptown local 1 train,
which is now running on the downtown
number 2 express track across the platform.
Return to 14th Street and begin again.
Have a nice day and thank you
for riding the MTA."

Dear Internal Revenue Service

Thank you for your letter informing me of the errors
in my 2005 filing. I'm enclosing a check for
$5,657 to cover the tax which I evidently
still owe and the interest on that tax.
I would hereby like to ask, however,
that you forgive the penalty of $1,136,
since the employer failed to send me a 1099
for the income I made as a consultant that year.
Of course I realize it's my responsibility to report
all my income, but in the absence of a 1099
I simply forgot. I have a number of clients
and I'm (obviously) not the best bookkeeper.
Nor am I particularly "good with money."
I am a poet as well as a freelance writer,
and being a poet isn't quite as lucrative
as you might imagine. You may notice,
for example, that for all of last year I received
$57 in royalties. (A friend of mine helpfully
observed that I could have made more money
"as a parking meter," to which I replied that
I could have made *a lot* more money as a parking meter,
and gotten a lot more respect as well.)
Unlike most hard-working poets in America,
I don't teach, mainly because I don't know anything.

I'm probably not all that far from the clichéd notion
of the romantic poet you yourself may hold.
I get stoned sometimes and stare at trees and clouds
for hours on end, try to *see* the wind, etc.
I weep for no reason, remember real or imagined
slights for ages, and lick my wounds with words.
I live in a studio apartment, a garret, if you will.
I have a huge desk—it's like the deck of a ship,
and I its landlocked captain, gazing out to sea.
It sits underneath my sleeping loft, which
my girlfriend likes to call "the lofty loft,"
for reasons I won't go into here as they may seem
inappropriate, or too personal, or perhaps
irrelevant to my purpose, which is to ask your
forgiveness of the penalty and to offer reasons why
by explaining the hardships of the poet's life.
I'll just say that sometimes it gets pretty lofty up there
and sometimes we imagine we're on a magic carpet
drifting smoothly above the city below, in its state
of semi-controlled, slow-motion collapse,
and on out over the ocean, which she loves and fears,
just like I do, or over the summer-campy Catskills,
where we can't afford to buy a country house,
with their worn-down mountains and charmingly
self-effacing trees, so unlike the impossibly massive
and overly serious cedars and hemlocks and
Douglas fir trees of the Pacific Northwest,

where I used to live until poverty forced me East.
Those trees are brooders—dignified, mist-shrouded
monsters—beautiful, of course, and awe-inspiring
(I wonder if you have felt this), but too damply
archaic and imposing and uncomprehendable
for my taste. I like a tree you can take in
with a single steady gaze. I wonder if you are
as bad at poetry as I am at accounting. Perhaps
we are the inverted mirror-images of each other.
I don't imagine you get asked that question
very often or receive many letters like this one.
Maybe you're reading this out loud even now
to your office (I almost said "cell") mates. Of my book
a reviewer once said that "one simply can't resist
reading these poems out loud to someone else,"
and I wonder if you feel this—the irresistible
need to read this poem aloud. I'm sure
the letters you receive are mostly angry ones,
the kind that say things like, "Here, take my
Goddamn money and buy Dick Cheney a few more
gallons of puppy blood for his nightly ablutions,"
or "Dear IRS, please use the enclosed check to
purchase some hand-held rocket-launchers to blast the fuck
out of some poor Iraqi's house, which you prefer
to call 'a suspected insurgent stronghold.'"
Or, "Please give this money to the CEO of Exxon
so he can buy silk socks while I regurgitate

my supper and try not to starve."
I thought of taking that approach, I felt
that desire to get in a shot or two, to give voice
to righteous indignation, treat you like
a nonperson, someone mindlessly
and heartlessly saying "no" all day long.
But I'm done with all that, I want to reach you,
to speak to you as a fellow human being immersed
in the same joys and suffering as I am—didn't you
once write poems yourself, poems of anguish
and loss and loneliness?—and to remind you
of the karmic delights of forgiveness that
await you if you release me
from this debt.

Fourth of July

Freedom is a rocket,
isn't it, bursting
orgasmically over
parkloads of hot
dog devouring
human beings
or into the cities
of our enemies
without whom we
would surely
kill ourselves
though they are
ourselves and
America I see now
is the soldier
who said I saw
something
burning on my
chest and tried
to brush it off with
my right hand
but my arm
wasn't there—
America is no

other than this
moment, the
burning ribcage,
the hand gone
that might have
put it out, the skies
afire with our history.

So Long

To break this day
free from all
the others

to stand at the
morning end
of it and

push off from
the shore
sail beyond

the reach of all
my failures
calling after me

"You can't just
leave us here"
shaking their fists

crowding into
the water
clamoring "We

made you who
you are" to
feel their voices

growing small
beneath
the surf

the wide un-
knowable ocean
all before me.

On the Subway Platform

for Kate

Where are you going I said
and she said I'm going

to look for a book
and I said what kind

of book? A book on
PERFECTIONISM

she said and I said
make sure you get

the right one—
which brought forth

such perfect laughter
from her perfect heart.

Over and Under

So sexy to slide under-
neath a river,
to sit inside this
snakelike sub-
marine-like
subway car and
freely imagine
the world above—
the Brooklyn
Bridge invisibly
trembling with the
weight of its
own beauty,
the East River
still guided by
the grooves
Walt Whitman's
eyes wore in it,
the bulldog tug-
boats pushing the
passively impressive
broad-bottomed
barges around,
and the double-

decker orange-
and-black Staten
Island ferries,
with their aura
of overworked
pack-mule
mournfulness,
and beyond them
the Atlantic Ocean
which I lately learned
was brought here
by ice comets three
billion years ago,
which explains
a few things, like
why everybody
feels so alienated,
and of course
the thoughts being
thought by every
person in New
York City at
this moment—
vast schools of
undulating fish
curving and rising
in the cloud-swirling

wind-waved sky,
surrounded by
the vaster emptiness
of nonthought
which holds them
and which they try
not to think
about and you
lying in bed in
your sixth-floor
walk-up sublet
on St. Mark's Place—
such a breath-
taking ascension!
imagining me
rising now to meet you.

To Make the Wound More Beautiful

George in New York

Inward, self-questioning, often unsure.
Often clearly miserable:
a kindred spirit, my nephew.
Readerly and melancholy.
The only other in my family
thus afflicted.
But the affliction is the way,
so I fed him books—
Salinger and Whitman,
the Greeks and ancient
Japanese poets,
Saigyō particularly.
Neruda of the odes,
of the wild undaunted
friendliness toward all things.
So that soon enough
he was taller than me,
handsomer, wiser,
gentler. When he came
to visit me in New York
I told him: "If I catch you
staring at the sidewalk

I'm sending you home."
After which he
noticed every bottle-
shard sculpture
in the East Village,
every brownstone gargoyle
in Park Slope.
Coming in from LaGuardia,
he'd tried to reason
the cabbie out of
a paranoid racist rant,
tried—between my shouts
and insults—calmly to
change his mind,
unwilling to give up
on anyone.
After I praised
his patience and intelligence,
he said he disliked
compliments, having inherited
the Midwestern
clairvoyance for all signs
of arrogance
in himself or others.
I knew that feeling well,
but I told him they're gifts,
it's ungracious not to

accept them.
And he seemed to accept that
and I complimented him
for doing so.
And then he shook off
his shyness like a fine black dust,
started talking to everyone—
jazz players after a set,
flea-market vendors,
fellow travelers on the subway.
Took his place in the world,
stepped into himself
and found he fit.
A wondrous thing to witness.
That will have been five
years ago this spring,
back when death was just an idea,
something to be spoken of
now and again.

———

My first thought when my brother called
was: This is going to happen and I
am going to die. When he called
from the hospital in Kyoto
to tell me George was worsening,
that his liver would fail,

that he needed a transplant
and I was the only viable donor—
my first thought was: This
is going to happen and I
am going to die.

And then I was on my way—
fearless and terrified,
watching a movie about
Dominican minor-leaguers
somewhere over the Pacific,
and life felt real, its strangeness
no longer half-hidden.
Six months before, I'd read a novel
about surgeons, its climactic scene
a harrowing, high-wire live
liver transplant between
twin brothers that saves
the recipient but kills the donor.
Why did I read that book,
why then? Past and future
inseparable, yes, I know.
But of all books I might
have read, why that book, why then?

———

First Meeting with the Surgeons

It was as if the helpless gods had convened
around a cluttered table to tinker
with fate one more time. I remember
how small the room seemed,
how unequal to tragedy or heroism,
the scuffled linoleum along the baseboards,
bookshelves overstuffed,
the unsteady chairs.
I remember Dr. Ogura,
the man who would cut me open
and delicately detach half my liver,
had a band-aid just above
his left eyebrow, and I wondered
had someone hit him, the parent
of a child who'd died in a failed
surgical procedure, a liver transplant
perhaps, or had he fallen
off his bicycle, or walked into
a doorjamb, or been gashed
by a low-hanging branch
while out for a Sunday stroll
in the hills above Kyoto?
You never see adults, or gods,
with band-aids on their faces,
but there he was, the injured surgeon.

And as he studied my blood tests
and explained the operation to me,
I couldn't stop thinking about it,
that cut above his eye, what
it looked like, how it happened,
what it might portend.

———

What is the sound of fear?

At Nijō Castle
the Shōgun not only

surrounded him-
self with thick

walls and deep moats

he built the floors
to sing like night-

ingales underfoot
to warn him

of an enemy's approach.

———

When they walked me into the surgical theater,
I thought: This will be a little foretaste

of death, or possibly death itself.
I had told my brother, "If George lives
and I die, I can live with that."

And the night before, after we visited him,
jaundiced and unconscious in the ICU
but still handsome enough to make
the nurses fall in love with him,
and had touched his forehead and
said encouraging words to him, who knew
nothing of what was about to happen,
unless the body always knows
and the deep mind that listens even
when the shallow mind is fast asleep—
we passed Dr. Ogura in the hall
and he asked me, "Are you ready?"
"Yes," I said. "Are *you?*"

But when the moment comes,
all bravura vanishes, you just surrender.
The last thing I remembered
as they held the mask above my face
to put me under, to induce "a reversible lack
of awareness" (a fair description
of the human condition), was a kind
young nurse smiling at me,
pumping her fists into the air,

as if in victory or exuberant bon voyage—
such a strange and beautifully incongruous image
before the world went dark.

———

Deep silence held him
and because he could not wake
I joined him there.

Nine hours our bodies lay
side by side, opened up,
while our absent spirits

did what? What did they do?
I like to think they
hovered together,

looked down on the carnage
below, the soft flesh
split apart, taken

and given, and that they forgave
each other for whatever
might happen,

held each other in the
dark and weightless ether
of the spirit world

before being called back
to the bloodied, bodied,
spinning world once more.

———

When his surgeon came to tell me, I was fussing
with a pillow, every move a whiplash of pain
and irritation. I felt my feet hanging
over the bed like two defeated fish, and thought:
This wasn't made for a six-foot-tall Nebraskan.
And could the room have been designed so that
a person recovering from major abdominal surgery
might turn the lights on and off without
getting gingerly in and out of bed? Certainly not.
Miserable with my tiny unmanageable miseries
when Dr. Ogura came in, sat down and said:
"I have some very bad news. George suffered
a massive cerebral hemorrhage. I'm afraid
there's nothing we can do. He's brain dead."

———

They couldn't control his blood,
they said, though my liver started
working immediately

in his body. His brain
was swamped with blood,
though my liver started working.

Nothing could be done, they said.
After all we did, nothing could
be done. Because his brain

was swamped with blood.
Even with half a liver working
perfectly, nothing could be done,

and nothing can be done
now there is a bloody swamp
where consciousness had been.

———

Sleepless every night since the operation
I wandered the halls of the transplant ward,
pushing the coatrack-like contraption
that held my IV-drip, pain-med drip,
and three electrodes affixed to my chest
to track my untrustworthy heart.
My midnight walks became in time
a kind of walking meditation.
Nothing like major surgery
to keep you attentive to every step.
Of course my mind was still the darting
school of panicked minnows it had
always been. But once, as I came
to the end of the hall and looked out
the darkened window, I imagined

a sleepless monk somewhere
in the hills beyond the city
doing his own walking meditation,
making the same slow circles,
he around some pond or towering pagoda
and I around thirty or forty wounded patients.
(In Japan an incision is a "wound.")
I imagined us mirroring each other,
like brothers, or like subatomic particles
split apart, apparently separate,
but spinning in perfect symmetry
no matter the space between.
I wondered if he was looking up
toward the hospital windows wondering
if someone there was thinking of him
and of the suffering we couldn't help but share.
And then I rounded the corner to begin
the long fluorescent journey
back to my room.

———

I wasn't there, but my brother told me
that after they cut him loose
from all the machines,
let his body go like a small boat
drifting from the shore,
as my brother and his wife

held vigil beside the bed,
the doctors and nurses
who had served and tried
to save him came into the room
and stood in stillness for over
an hour until it was over—
until the strong young heart
stopped. He had been brain dead
for ten days but still with us,
rocking gently on the surface.
And then they all rode
the elevator down together,
the same elevator
we had taken up so many times,
big enough for gurneys and wheelchairs
and huge anxious silences.
And when his body had been
placed inside the hearse
that waited to enter the flurried stream
of Maratumachi Street, they
bowed a long low bow, held it
until the car was gone.

I knelt beside his body the night before
we would consign it to the flames,
and read his journals, read his poems:

may my foot find your doorstep,
that is why I walk each day

may my hand move with yours,
that is why I write

may I come home to your knowing,
that is why I live

How perfect and unlikely that death
should draw us together here in Kyoto,
where he'd come to teach and where
the poet we loved most, Saigyō, lived
and was cast out and wandered
these mountains in loneliness and rapture,
Saigyō, the warrior turned monk, who wrote:

> *"Detached" observer*
> *of blossoms finds himself in time*
> *intimate with them—*
> *so, when they separate from the branch,*
> *it's he who falls . . . deeply into grief.*

So strange to think
a piece of me is already
buried in the air,

or exists as ashes
in an urn
mixed with his ashes,

and that when I'm ready
to make the final turn,
step through
the final wound
and leave this body,
part of me will be waiting there.

From One Place to Another

We sat in the Yamatoya Jazz Bar,
such an unlikely place, dark
and soothing, deep in Kyoto,
its decor a cross between
a whorehouse and a 1970s
American basement—
red lampshades with gold
tassels, mismatched
sofas and chairs,
and thousands of LPs
shelved along red velvet walls.
My brother asked for Ellington,
"Take the A Train," by the shy,
continuously inspired
Billy Strayhorn.
Can you make a song
from instructions on
how to get from one place
to another? Yes.
Beer and ginger ale
is what we were drinking,
New York City what we
were thinking of—
my brother and I at The Fez

to hear the Mingus Big Band,
George and I at Barbès
to hear a Django guitarist.
Weeping is what we
were not doing, no elbows
on knees, faces in hands,
shoulders heaving—no,
we were taking a break
from all that, taking the A train
uptown to Harlem,
we stepped right up onto it
laughing as it lurched away
from the station nearly
knocking us down.

———

Hobbled up
narrow cobble-
stone lanes
to the Pure
Land Buddhist
Temple
its haloed
half-smiling
Amitabha Buddha
perfectly placed
at the edge

of the graveyard
his hands
forming the
teaching mudra
as if to say
take heed
wake up
death comes
without warning.
Yes it does
I thought as I
looked out
over Kyoto
its thousand
ancient temples
and million
cramped apart-
ments—a city
like all cities
of the living
and dying
living together
side by side
one and the same.

Leaning over Sanjō Bridge
in mossy August light,
I imagine him
leaning here, looking
down on the lonely
Kamo River.
Maybe he saw the same
thin white crane
that stands and looks and
needles the shallow water.
Or another just like it.
Maybe he said to himself,
as I did: *so they do
exist outside Zen paintings.*
But where would he
have been going,
crossing this bridge from
one side to the other?
What thinking?
The smell of being alone
in a strange city—
would he have noticed that?
One more thing there is now
no way of knowing.

At Kiyomizu Temple
tourists clown
for the cameras

line up to catch
in a long-handled cup
its falling healing waters.

———

How I longed to be home—
such a roomy word:
"home." And here

I am

in this emptiness
with nothing to do but
rest and think and remember.

Ultrasound

"Well," she said, "your incision is huge."
Yes, I wanted to say, I noticed that.
Or: You should see the other guy.
Though I did wonder how much bigger
than other scars my scar must have been
to shock a sixty-something radiologist.
Then she greased my crucified torso
and slid the camera over me
to photograph the lightning storms of pain
the thirteen hour flight from Osaka
to Denver had unleased again.
"The left lobe of your liver is gone," she said.
"There's nothing there." OK, I thought,
tell me something I *don't* know.
And then she did: "Did you have
a gallbladder before this surgery?"
"As far as I know," I said. "Well," she said,
"you don't have one now." "Jesus," I said,
my vast ignorance of the body surging up
into speech. "Can you live without that?"
"Oh, sure," she said, "you don't need it.
People have them taken out all the time."
But then I wondered what else
the doctors in Kyoto failed to tell me,

or I failed to hear. Did I still have
an appendix, for example, or my tail-less
tailbone? Or any other ancillary
or vestigial organs the body
may have been born with?
And what about my totally superfluous
sense of impending doom? Or the not
strictly necessary or useful everlastingness
of all my wounds and regrets? Or my feeling
that failure might be a natural element
like water or air? Those were not removed,
were they? I don't think I could part
with them just yet.

Update

Six months later
it's still the same:
I wake at 2 a.m.
my body hyper-
vigilant, as if
to say: *Don't
cut me again.*
And the sleep
meds—Restoril,
Valium, Lunesta,
Ambien? Candy
to my fearsome
sleeplessness.
They only make
me wish I had
the job of giving
drugs their names—
(a poet should
have that job)
like Adam
in the pharma-
ceutical garden.

Dr. Ogura

I'm glad I wasn't conscious
when they stapled me shut.
Do they use a staple gun?

No . . . and yet they must.
How else get them in?
I should have asked,

I guess, or possibly not.
But when Dr. Ogura took
them out, so skillfully

I could hardly feel it—
fifty-six of them clamped
along the incision

he'd opened—I asked him
why they used staples now
instead of stitches.

He paused, his hand poised
above my abdomen, then pulled
from his imperfect English

a perfect reply: "To make
the wound . . . more beautiful."

One moment keeps drifting back
above all the others,
unloosened from time's illusory flow:

how he stood in the Met
mesmerized before Van Goghs
and Monets and Pissaros,

as if held by some distant signal
from the source of beauty itself,
and asked in a breathless whisper,
Are those the originals?

FROM *No Day at the Beach*
(2020)

Back Then

Everything was better back then.
Even my nostalgia was better,
more piercing, more true.
I miss missing things that much,
but not as much as I missed
missing things back then.
Even my anxieties about the future,
which have indeed come to pass,
were more vivid back then,
more real. Reality itself seemed
more real back then—this clanking
stage-play only a fool could find
convincing—I fell for it all,
and it killed me, again and again.
Ghosts of myself wander
the cities I've lived in, thinking
of other cities, imagining me
here imagining them.
We nod to each other across
the years, the way the last line
of a poem will sometimes
look back, wistfully,
at the first.

Tough Town

Squirrels
knocked

it down
three

days
ago but

a puffed-
up finch

keeps
staring

at where
the bird-

feeder
used to be.

Swifts

for my father

Early fall, the light thin and brittle, and if
it's true that deprivation is a gift,
I accept the gift. I walk down
to Wallace Park to watch the swifts
that roost every September
in the Chapman School's tall
brick chimney. The charming swifts
with their long, forked tails
and swept-back wings,
ten thousand of them swerving
and darting in the evening sky,
a flowing, expandable spiral
of birds, clearing the air of insects
and riveting the wandering
human mind. Tonight there must be
three hundred spectators,
a whole hillside of us, ordinary people
whose wings fell off eons ago,
who traded flight for speech
and have regretted it ever since,
sodden and earth-bound as we are,

except for our lifted eyes, our *oohs* and *ahs*
that show we're still alive when
the peregrine falcon dives in
and knifes one out of the air,
which we boo or cheer,
sometimes simultaneously.
We love this passion play of form
and formlessness,
the birds' shifting patterns
flung out like a whiplash of water
or school of fish above
the stationary human school,
then drawn tight together,
a miracle they don't crash into each other,
a miracle of echolocation, until
you see them as they truly are:
a single organism, a body made mostly
of air and quick decisions, jagged
motions that gradually cohere—
a poem, in other words.
It takes the flock a full twenty minutes
to funnel down into the chimney,
and it seems a living smoke
pulled back into a still and sleeping fire,
so beautiful I forget for a moment
my father's death, or I turn my mind
away from it or, no, I open

my grief to accommodate this wonder
and wonder what he might have thought of it,
were we standing here together,
the kind of thing we never did, and now
will never do, except in my imagination—
that unchanging inner sky where the swifts
take flight whenever I want them to
and my father cannot die.

Sleeping in the Wind

> *it is a mistake*
> *being incarnate*
> —*Lucia Perillo*

How beautiful it will be to be
a wind without a body,
a swift unfolding curvature
of air, slightly lighter,
or heavier, than standing air,

flickering a candleflame in Tibet
or tousling the hair
of a woman falling in love;
carrying off the stench
of a massacre, dissolving it,

then coming back cleanly to be
breathed by murderers and
mourners alike. Is that
what it will be like—
after this creaking sideshow

we watch from the cheap seats
of ourselves, the hands
crippling up, in constant pain,
the back proving the foolishness
of walking upright again

and again, the trees still calling us
to live up there, safely out
of sight, at ease above the earth,
harmless and free from these
imperfect accommodations,

caressed by and sleeping in
the wind we will become?

Fedora

I have a sweaty, hat-ruining head.
My straw fedora sports a ring
of darkish discoloration
around the brim.
Luckily I'm tall, so only God
can see it and it hardly
bothers Him,
though it worries me.
It's on my list of things
to worry about: money,
relationships, my career, *ha!*,
the jittery hummingbird
of my heart, the shocking
scarcity of jazz clubs
here in Portland, Oregon,
(why, oh why, did I leave
New York?), my father's dying,
my mother's loneliness.
Sweat stains on my hat
sometimes rise
to the top of the list.
Which shows what kind
of person I am, frivolous
and vain, though I like

to think myself otherwise.
I wear the fedora even
when hiking in the high heat
of summer, knowing it will make
the sweat stains worse.
Why? Because a beautiful woman
once smiled at me on the trail,
and I'm sure it was partly
due to my hat, so stylish
and unexpectedly debonair
in the bright green forest.
She was not tall. She could not see
what my worrisome head
had done to it.

Falling Hours

No one can tell how
the metaphors we live by
may be fulfilled.
Five years ago I lay
with my belly
cut open, in Kyoto,
surrounded by surgeons—
nine hours
plunged into
memoryless darkness,
my nephew
lying next to me.
They lifted half
my tender, viscous liver,
held it like a fish pulled from
the ocean depths
of the body,
and gave it to him,
a gift he did not refuse
but which would
not save him.
I remember
the sleepless night before,
walking down

to the 24-hour
convenience store
in the hospital basement
to buy a clock so I could watch
the hours fall away,
the last hours
of my life as someone
who had merely *felt*
cut open.
The hallways empty,
3 a.m. fluorescent lights
in the transplant ward
giving off
a frazzled hum
of desolation,
the nurse
at the nurses' station,
her eyebrows popping up
like question marks
when she saw me
pass by.
I still have the clock,
silver and black and cheaply made,
(plastic, not brass or steel),
but trustworthy nonetheless.
It has a button
on the side you can press

to light up its face
so you can see
the time
in the darkness.
That clock was there—
it held those hours
in its dominion,
its hands
swept through them.
I keep it on my nightstand
like something
brought back from a dream
to prove
that it was real.

Signs and Wonderings

When I see the inevitable bad puns of hair salons
—*Hair Apparent*, *A Cut Above*, *Hair Force*,
Julius Scissor, *Hair We Are*, etc.—I think
how painful it must be to answer the phone:
"*Curl Up and Dye*, how can I help you?"
Well, you can start by changing the name
of your salon to something simple like *Shirley's
Style and Cut*, or *Pam's Perms*, or *Main Street
Hair Salon*, and leave the puns to professionals
like myself who once impressed everyone
at a rooftop party in Brooklyn when a colleague
asked, "Do the French roll their *R*s?" and I said,
"They roll their *eyes*." Or when at the Indian
restaurant, I said, "We could start with some *naan*,
but that would be a *naan starter*," which has
the virtue of being both a pun and paradox.
A professor of mine in grad school once said:
"A pun is two words competing for the same
semantic space." Yes, but why must everything
be a competition? Or a question of space,
of trying to occupy or empty it? "What kind of pie
are you having today, sir?" "I'm having the occu-pie."
"How is it?" "It's terrible, but it fills me up."
And is that what we all want, to be filled up,

with food or words or love or hatred or memories?
With ideas, beliefs, opinions? Of what use are they?
I used to think I wanted to be empty, but once
on magic mushrooms I felt my mind was being
sucked out of my head, pulled into the void,
and it terrified me. I very much wanted that
not to happen. "Ego death," I later learned,
was how Terence McKenna described the experience,
which makes me wish I'd surrendered to it, gone
through that portal into shimmering dissolution,
to re-emerge—as what? More open, more awestruck,
less tightly clenched around my fears and desires?
Now I imagine actual death, or try to.
The mind can't really conceive its nonexistence,
can't create a space where it enacts its own undoing.
But to think of death, to write about it, is that
a way to call it forth? Does death listen to us,
cock its ear like a dog when it hears us
speak its name? I wondered about that last night,
after reading about the brilliant young neurosurgeon
who gets lung cancer and knows he's going to die
and has to tell himself all the things he told
his patients. I tell myself—I tell others, too—
that I'm not afraid of death, but last night it felt
more real, that it's going to happen, that I won't
be *me* anymore, won't be here, or anywhere.
It was as if death had heard me and said, "Oh, really?

Not afraid? Are you *sure*?" Here in Oregon
trees compete for the same space and life
and death are intertwined, rooted together,
entangled in earth and air, as a seed will fall
on a fallen tree, a Douglas fir or cedar
or redwood, some mossy beast lying prone
beside a ravine, and begin to rise up, drawing on
the nutrients of the trunk decomposing beneath it,
an opportunist we might say, lifting itself into the sky.
And sometimes when the dead tree is wholly gone,
has become air, the space it occupied will remain,
an opening, a reminder of where death became life,
and the new tree's roots reach down, drip down,
around that emptiness to hold itself upright for,
if it's lucky, a few hundred years. I leave it to you
to grasp the implications, the possibilities for
metaphor, in this unfolding forest parable. But now,
as the year is ending, I wonder if time itself works
that way—one day, or week, or year, or moment,
growing out of the death of the previous one,
or if the dissolution of individual consciousness
at death nourishes a larger consciousness,
or if the spirit, the breath-spirit, is released at last
to fly around and observe with infinite
compassion the infinite folly of the living,
perhaps now and then to intervene.
Impossible questions! But maybe I'll call

the *Curl Up and Dye* hair salon
and ask them just the same.

Blathery Performance

Sometimes the ego is a one-man marching band,
high-stepping down main street, pounding a bass drum
with one hand, mouth-farting through a tuba
        with the other.
That's how I feel, anyway, when I look back at some
of my blathery performances, where I sharpen my wit
on other people's weaknesses, reel off judgments
and opinions like decrees, jump on every opportunity
to say something funny, however hurtful it might be.
When I asked a friend to give me the gossip
about a certain writers workshop
where I teach once a year, she said there's
tension around who has to drive visiting authors
to and from the airport and she doesn't want
to do it anymore. "That's it?" I said.
"Friction over who has to pick up the big shots
from the airport? That's all you've got?"
Laughing, but really looking for conflict,
intrigue, gross incompetence, juicy misconduct,
while silently noting that no one offers to drive *me*.
And then I launched into my spiel about MFA
programs, their plenitude, the dependency they
spawn, churning out poets by the hundreds
every year. "We don't need any more poets,"

I said. "We have more than enough already."
I tossed off Philip Larkin's remark about how
he missed the days when writing poetry was slightly
disreputable and you had to hide your notebook
under the bed when somebody knocked at the door.
I trotted out my anecdote about giving a talk
at the AWP conference on finding work
outside academia and how a young woman,
a recent graduate from an MFA program,
raised her hand to express her anxiety that
without a workshop and prompts and deadlines,
she wouldn't be able to write, and my first thought
was, well, in that case, YOU'RE NOT A WRITER.
Of course I didn't say that then, but here I was
proudly proclaiming my un-empathic thought,
holding up my meanness as if it were wisdom.
And then quoting Flannery O'Connor who,
when asked if she thought universities
were stifling young writers, replied:
"They don't stifle enough of them."
At this point, my friend frowned a little,
but did that slow me down? Not at all.
I pulled out another practiced remark about
how in America anything worth doing
is worth overdoing and if having twenty
MFA programs is good, 200 is even better!
And thus the glut of mediocre writers,

with the unspoken implication that all this
noise was drowning out the brilliance
of my own work. Young people shouldn't
be encouraged to write poetry, I said.
No one encouraged *me* to become a poet,
certainly not my parents, who thought it was
a bizarre waste of time and suggested I learn
a trade instead, and look how well I turned out.
The conversation went on in this vein for some time,
and you may notice that while I seem to be
proffering these harsh judgments as examples of ego
run amok, and thus disavowing them, I am also
giving voice to them and secretly hoping
you'll agree with at least some of them.
And then I announced that I had just been
accepted into a mindfulness meditation
teacher training program, and how excited I was
to be moving into a new kind of teaching,
bringing my spiritual practice and my poetry
into greater alignment, how I planned to offer
a weekly poetry and meditation class.
I could not feel the angels of irony looking
down on me as I said this, but I feel them now,
raising their angelic eyebrows, scratching
their celestial chins, wondering how anyone
so mired in judgment could possibly
teach mindfulness. Maybe you should try

practicing it first, I can almost hear them thinking.
And now I see that in describing/confessing
my obsessive, relentless self-concern,
I am really seeking affirmation for my honesty
and that in admitting this hidden motive
I am further promoting an image of myself
as a person of fearless self-awareness,
and so on and so forth down the infinite
hall of mirrors that is the ego and its sly
maneuverings. Ah, the ego, it won't enjoy
being spoken of in this way, pinned to the page,
undercut, exposed, its bag of tricks revealed.
Even now it's angling for an advantage,
trying to make a comeback, looking for a way to end
this poem that will bring praise, applause, a prize,
maybe even a ride to the airport. Which is
not going to happen.

I Decided to Weigh My Head

Was it really as heavy as it felt?
I got the scale out
from under the bathroom sink.
That's where it lives,
tilted on its side,
resting in its zeroes.
Would my head weigh more
than the *Collected Works
of Anthony Trollope*?
More than my overfed
tuxedo cat?
Would my jittery thoughts
balance out
my mournful ones?
Or would my head reveal itself
to be largely empty, like
the universe,
which it contains,
as I'd often feared
and sometimes wished?
I realized I would need a mirror.
I lay down
on the bathroom tile,
pillowed the scale

under the back of my skull,
held the hand mirror at arm's length
and took a good look
at myself,
the absurdity of my situation,
a grown man lying
between toilet and tub
wearing the slightly
self-mocking
anticipatory expression
of a person who has decided
to weigh his head.
The number floated above me
as in a thought-bubble
and I had my answer: 8.8 lbs.,
two infinities
turned rightside up,
the eightfold path doubled,
the number of years my father lived
minus the decimal,
and about half as heavy
as I'd imagined
this thing my spine had evolved
to lift into the air and carry
above the earth
would be.

Genius Offshore

Standing in the
ocean

calm for
a long while

when three
big ones

lift me up
knock me

down and
I realize even

the waves
come in waves.

No Day at the Beach

It's no day at the beach
being me, I said.
It's no walk
in the park.
I can see that,
she said.
Trust me, I said.
It's no picnic.
Clearly, she said.
What's that
supposed
to mean? I said.
I'm just agreeing
with you, she
said. You might
have argued
a bit, I said. Tried
to convince me
otherwise.
Who knows,
maybe it *is*
a day at the beach
being me. Or
maybe it's a day

at the beach
being *with* me.
No, she said. It's not.

Sightlines

We'll have to shear off the tops of those trees
if they continue to block my view
of the mountain. Not only our trees
but the neighbors' as well. Find some
daredevil to fly a helicopter upside
down over the neighborhood
and give it a good haircut.
It's America, people will do anything.
And my sightline is sacrosanct.
I need to see that peak floating
like Fuji, not just know it's there.
So I can orient my immaterial
longings, my desire to transcend
earthly limitations. I can't be
expected to pray to something
half obscured by these lesser gods
etching themselves into the evening air,
performing their fantastic
collaborations with the wind, keeping
or dropping their needles or leaves,
subject as they are to time and change.
What can they teach me about how to be?

The Empty Chair

Waiting for the poetry reading
to get started, I turn around
to apologize to the man
sitting diagonally behind me
for blocking his view.
I am tall, the back of my head
has absorbed a thousand
silent curses at movies, concerts,
theatrical performances, etc.
But he says it's OK,
thanks me for my kindness.
My friend sitting next to me
offers to switch seats
so I can stretch my legs
into the aisle but I say no,
if I sat there I'd *really* block his view—
unless my head were to become
suddenly transparent,
which I wish it would do,
the solid self, the illusion
of the solid self, gone:
just eyes and ears to see
and hear with, otherwise
vacant space, clean, open, clear,

like a window a breeze
blows into, billowing
the white diaphanous curtains,
and there's an empty chair
where a man once sat
reading, thinking, thinking
of nothing, offering no
obstruction, nothing to obstruct.

Intrigue in the Trees

Horse-collared by the high heat
of mountainous afternoons,
dogged by furious
dissatisfactions,
snakebit, buffaloed,
bird-brained. Thank you,
animals, for giving us so many
useful metaphors, and forgive
us for disappearing you,
daily and eternally.
Often I wonder:
is the earth trying to get
rid of us, shake us off,
drown us, scorch us
to nothingness?
To save itself and all other
creatures slated for destruction?
The trees around here
seem friendly enough—
stoic, philosophically inclined
toward nonjudgmental
awareness and giving
in their branchings
perfect examples

of one thing becoming two
and remaining one—
but who knows
what they really feel?
Just last night I was walking
to my favorite café,
The Laughing Goat,
when I saw a murder of crows
circling raincloudy sky,
arguing, speaking strangely,
suddenly alight on
a maple tree, dozens of them
closing down their wings
like arrogant, ill-tempered
magistrates. Everybody
was looking up and
watching. Some kind of
consultation was happening there
(animals think we're crazy
for thinking they can't think),
and I said to a woman
passing in the crosswalk:
I wonder what they're
planning. She laughed and
kept right on going,
happy as a lark.

In Brooklyn

a whoosh
of wind

whipped
my hat

right off
spun it up–

ward thirty
feet in air

my black
felt fedora

no driver
would stop

or even
swerve for

on rush hour
Flatbush

Avenue—
there it was

high above
the street

flopping and
leaping

like an
erratic over-

excited kite
or like the

thoughts it sits
on top of

as if my mind
had tried

to fly away
(where

would it
go?) and

taken my hat
with it but

the wind
dropped it

at my feet
unharmed

like Dorothy
after the

tornado—
I clamped

it on my
head and

crossing the
crosswalk

counted
it a miracle.

Etiquette

Here in New
York City

smiling is
frowned

upon and
looking

up looked
down upon.

Greatness

I fell asleep at the great poet's reading last night.
It was such a pleasure to feel myself slipping
off the blurred and queenly self-importance
of her words into blissful wandering dream-state,

my chin bouncing off my chest once or twice
and not to resist the unconsciousness
she seemed almost deliberately to inspire.

At the applause I awoke refreshed.
That was great, I said, and the man sitting
in front of me said, Yes, it doesn't get
much better than that.

Nebraska

After watching
Nebraska

a film shot
entirely

in black
& white

in my
home state

I told my
friend as

the credits
rolled

"You know,
they shot

that in
color, that's

just what
Nebraska

looks
like" and

he said
"Really?"

and I said
"Jesus, no,

man,"
secretly

happy he
considered it.

Walk the Talk

Sometimes
I think

human
beings

are just
a way

for words
to walk

around
on earth

and
words

just a way
for wind

to hear
itself think.

Field of Vision

Our survival cost us our happiness,
always scanning for lions
stalking the open

savannahs—is that
a panther or just wind
in the tall grass moving?

The careless became
a big cat's satisfied sleep.
The rest of us are here,

five million years of fear
hard-wiring our brains
to be on guard, to look

for trouble, for the one
thing wrong with this picture,
whatever the picture might be.

Now we do it out of habit,
even when there's no reason,
when we're perfectly safe,

walking out each morning
under the baobab trees, naked,
into the lion's field of vision.

Dick's Kitchen Metaphysical

When I set aside the book about knowledge
of higher worlds and how to attain it,
dog-earing the passage that explains
why the initiate must listen without
judgment to whatever is being said,
however contrary or noxious it might be,
the waitress at Dick's Kitchen asks me
if I'm still "working on everything."
And I answer "yes" because I'm not only
lingering over my turkey burger
and sweet yam "not fries" but pondering
questions of life and death and how to
access the mystical realm that shimmers
like a heat mirage at the center of all things.
But when she further inquires if my food
"is still tasting well," I feel myself plummeting
back into the lower worlds where all I do
is silently correct my fellow human beings
for the way they dress or drive or speak or think,
peppering them with sarcastic questions
or barking at them in my head like
a full-blown crazy person: *HOW COULD
YOU VOTE FOR THAT APOPLECTIC
ORANGE-FACED RACIST IGNORAMUS?*

or *OH FOR THE LOVE OF CHRIST YES YOU*
CAN TURN RIGHT ON RED THAT'S BEEN
A RULE FOR ABOUT FIFTY YEARS
I GUESS THEY FORGOT TO TELL YOU!
But then I remember the section on
patience, forbearance, and nonanger,
(which I had been tempted to skip), that says:
"Every symptom of impatience produces
a paralyzing effect on the higher faculties."
And suddenly I see them, my higher faculties,
frozen like statues, in attitudes of agony
and strife, like Rodin's prisoners
or Michelangelo's slaves, wisdom languishing
in chains, compassion with downcast eyes,
kindness struggling to rise
from the stone.

Here: An Epithalamion

Before I met you my life was, as you know,
no day at the beach. For every victory,
ten defeats; for every joyful moment,
a melancholy week; for every shapely
poem, a thick volume of silence.
I was always pining for some
golden age, thinking everything
was better back then, even
my nostalgia was better, more
piercing, more true. Wherever I was
I wanted to be somewhere else,
but when I got there I wanted to be
back where I started. Now I know
that what I wanted was to be here,
with you, though I had only a sliver of faith
I would ever find you, just a feather
from the bird of hope. I was a glass
half broken kind of person. Ken Pallack
gave me a racehorse nickname,
Stagedoor Johnny, which I quickly
changed to *Trapdoor Johnny*, and
dropped right through it.
I thought I was who I thought I was.
And when I tried to embrace

my imperfections, even my arms
fell short. And all the false starts,
wrong turns, convoluted detours,
and treacherous conditions! It seems
I had to fail at love every possible way
to make the way possible for you.
But now you're here and here is where
I want to be. Frank O'Hara said
"It is easy to be beautiful; it is
difficult to appear so." But not for you,
you're beautiful all the way through,
no disharmony between essence
and appearance, and I love you
from the touch of your skin to
the depths of your soul, and I would
gladly embrace your imperfections
if you had any, and Joseph Goldstein
says anything can happen anytime
and that's true, but only *this* could be
happening right now, only this moment,
which is the fruit of the tree of every moment
that came before it, the secret momentum
that brought me to you and you to me
and all of us here to this garden—
only *this* moment, which as I write it
I can only imagine but as I say it
is really happening, a miracle,

right here, right now, lifted up
from time's unrelenting flow
and held within the loving sphere
of all our friends and family:
here, now, just this, forever.

Over the Moon

for Alice

Five a.m.—the soft percussion of the rain
on the slanted rooftop of my study.
I study it: a single drop dropping again
and again at one second intervals,
like the ticking of a watery clock
above my head. Off to my right,
it comes down in loose clusters,
an absent-minded thrumming of fingers
on a tabletop, random, irregular,
or falling in a pattern I can't perceive.
It's too dark to see the rain as it falls,
only the reflection of my room
projected onto the empty space beyond
my *window*—an old Norse word
made from two other words: *wind* and *eye*.
My bookcases float blurrily
in the air above the alley,
I tap the keyboard and words appear,
and now the rain appears to be hesitating,
or reconsidering, though it will likely
fall all day long on the bamboo trees

I cannot see, the glorybower, the lilacs
and azaleas readying themselves,
summoning their flowers from the depths
of nonexistence, three kinds of Japanese
maples and the improbable ferns,
huge and flamelike, heart-shaped,
that edge the yard. Last night we stopped
and stepped backward when we crossed
a sidewalk puddle where the moon
had fallen between a reflection
of rootlike branches and swiftly
passing clouds to hover underneath us.
As above, so below, the old alchemists said,
everything mirroring everything else,
falling and rising and falling.
We lingered looking down, then
stepped over the moon and came home.

FROM *Dharma Talk*
(2023)

Morning Dilemma

Awake at four this morning.
Why, I'm not sure.
Outside it's dark and rainy.
Nothing's visible beyond
a few sketchy trees,
a white fluorescent streetlight
one block over like
a chunk of moon lodged in
winter branches. A day to stay
inside and read a novel
about almost-human robots.
Thank God for novelists.
Old age would be
insupportable without them.
Meditate, read novels,
write poems now and then,
stare out the window,
love my wife: that's my plan
for growing old.
My ambition. A ladybug
walked across my desk
a few minutes ago.
Do they fly around in the cold
rain of December? I considered

sliding a piece of paper
under it, opening the window,
and flicking it into
the outer darkness, like a word
flying off a page, but wondered
if it might prefer to stay inside
where it's warm and dry.
And in any case, I would
have had to dislodge my cat,
and she had one foreleg
draped over her eyes,
as if the world were already
too much to bear, which it is,
and while I was struggling
with that decision, the ladybug
moved itself out of my
field of vision, eliminating
the problem without solving it.
Such was the morning's drama
and dilemma—
darkness outside, a visitor
from the insect world, isolated
sharp light illuminating
a chalice of stripped branches,
a man with a cat on his lap
considering it all.
Who's to say we weren't

a single being in that moment,
a moment of miraculous
consciousness spread across,
bestowed upon, arising from
these things I have seen and
named and briefly touch
with my mind before
the day begins.

Sleep Thief

My wife had the brilliant idea
to put jasmine blossoms
beside the bed
to help carry me off
to sleep and keep me there
all night long—
sleep, blessed sleep,
like the elegant doe
you catch sight of
in the forest and then
it bounds away
—but in the night
my cat ate my wife's
brilliant idea
and stepped right over
my spinning head
and curled herself into
a black spiral
of unimpeded slumber
and thought nothing of it.

Wishful Thinking

I wish I could lift my brain
from my skull, rest it
in a bowl of cool water,
watch the steam rise,
listen to it sizzle—the poor,
reckless, overheated thing,
always worrying, always wanting.
I would bathe it in sea salt
and lavender, rose oil
and eucalyptus, cradle it
against my chest like a child,
this thing crazed and crafted
by five million years of fear,
the lions that stalked us
on the African savannahs
now internalized.

In its place would be
a space where nothing
could happen,
an attic room with pitched
ceilings and dormer windows
looking out on falling snow,
elm trees etched into

a metallic winter sky,
absolute silence.

A dream house, warm
enclosure and cold clarity
sailing into the wind,

no one at the helm.

Wanting Not Wanting

I wish I didn't
want things

to be other
than they are

but wanting
to be some-

one who
doesn't want

things to be
other than

they are is
just another

way of wanting
things to be

other than
they are—

and I don't
want that.

Dharma Talk

He said changing nothing changes
everything, which if you change

the words around also suggests
that changing everything

changes nothing,
which further implies

that nothing and everything
are interchangeable, are

in fact the same thing, or
the same non-thing, having

no fixed, unchanging nature,
or a nature that is in constant

change, if change can be said
to be constant, and is therefore

a kind of emptiness about
which it is better to speak

only in the negative, of
what it is not, or not

to speak at all.

Emptiness Is Not Enough

"Emptiness is not enough," you said,
and we all laughed at that, filling the air
with an ancient human sound.
Funny how we never think
of hunter-gatherers laughing,
but they must have, all that time
lying around singing and fucking,
there must have been laughter, too—
monkey business, Paleolithic slapstick.
Has anyone studied the evolution
of laughter, of humor? Probably.
Is there anything we *haven't* studied,
haven't dragged into the realm of
human comprehension? Even
emptiness: whole books on it,
many talks, six-week online courses,
nine-day retreats. Not that we will
ever know all there is to know
about the empty knowing that pervades
all things. Some neuroscientists
now believe the only way to solve
"the hard problem of consciousness,"
how we get from unconscious matter
to subjective awareness, is by positing

that all matter is, to one degree or another,
conscious, and that human consciousness
is just a scaling up (in some cases
a scaling down) of the consciousness
that's already present in trees and grass, ants
and antelope. Panpsychism is what such
a philosophical position is called, a modern
version of what our distant ancestors
knew to be true, that everything is alive
with spirit, intelligence, sacredness.
Still, one might ask why matter is conscious,
why is there consciousness at all?
An unanswerable question, also known
as a mystery. But why am I saying all this,
suddenly giving a little lecture on a subject
I can just barely pretend to almost understand?
Infinite causes and conditions brought me
to this moment, who can untangle them?
Last night, just before sleep, I prayed
for inspiration, for a poem to be given to me,
and this is what has arisen from the emptiness,
the shape my wish has taken. That would be
one way to explain it. The other ways
are beyond me.

Flight Path

Steadiness
is a virtue

yes but un-
steadiness

also has
its uses—

the butterfly's
wobbly

flight for
example

which is its
only defense

against
predators

like my cat
who leaps

and swipes
and misses

unable
to track its

jagged
trajectory—

how did
nature know

to embody
such perfectly

calibrated
imperfections

in this dreamy
creature

Chuang-Tzu
dreamt of

or was dreamt
up by so

long ago and
which I

(possibly
also my cat)

am dreaming
of now?

The Things We Tell Each Other

Now that the sky blurs to a sulfurous, apocalyptic yellow,
filled with what our ancient forests have become,
smoke and ash, ghost and accusation,
the constant nerve-grinding flight of helicopters
that ruined every possible silence—aerial tours,
life flights, police surveillance?—has finally ceased.
And so there is one silver lining to our charred
nightmare, the others remain to be seen.
A friend said, *I think it's good the earth
is getting rid of the inflammation inside her.
Unfortunate that life on the outside has to suffer.*
Another said something about *burning through
our karma.* As if finding the right metaphor
would make it all make sense, turn it into an idea,
something to be thought about, cool to the touch.
United in their muted anger, even the crows are quiet.
Houses half a block away slip into the unseen,
and the dreamlike nature of reality
the Buddha spoke about now seems quite real,
no longer hidden, though of course nothing
is what it seems, not even our illusions.
I drove down from the mountain the night
the fires started, through darkened towns strewn
with branches, power out, stoplights blank, wind

shaking the car, and I felt I was watching it all happen
from a distance, nightly news coverage of a routine disaster
involving other people, except that I was in it this time.
My contemplations on impermanence have not
been deep enough, apparently, because whole towns
dematerializing overnight, a million acres scorched,
fifty thousand people fleeing in terror, still seems
like something that should not be happening.
But the curandero says *the universe knows what it's doing*,
and *the collective awakening is a done deal.*
It's beautiful, the things we tell each other,
the things we think to say. All I know is that
I've been working on this poem for four days
and now the smoke has almost cleared.
The sky is open for business. The choppers are back.

Metta

The book I'm reading suggests we send
lovingkindness to everyone we see,
silently addressing them thus:
"May you be well, may you be safe,
may you be happy." And I do this
for a while, sitting inside a café,
watching the foot traffic go by.
It feels good—generous,
loving, kind. But after a time
I start modifying the blessing:
"May you be well, may you be safe,
may you be happy . . . and maybe also
lose the frowning-into-the-phone
facial expression I get so tired
of seeing everywhere I go."
It's the shadow side of lovingkindness
sticking its nose in, having its say,
and I can't seem to shut it up.
Someone else walks by and I offer:
"May you be well, may you be safe,
may you be happy . . . and while you're at it,
how about some nicer clothes?
It wouldn't kill you to dress
with a bit more panache, would it?"

I keep on in this way, dishing out
blessings with a side of helpful advice,
until I notice across the room two young women
sitting side by side, talking quietly,
in no need of either my good wishes
or my corrective commentary.
But then I see that one of them is crying,
nodding her head when her friend
says something, wiping tears
from her cheeks with the palms
of her hands. She pulls it together
for awhile, but then her face clenches
and she gives in, until her friend
lays a hand on her shoulder
and she can talk again—a gentle
rhythm of crying and talking,
waves rising and falling.
It doesn't look like she's been
visited by tragedy, a sudden death
or shattering diagnosis.
Ordinary heartbreak would be
my guess, the shock of betrayal,
some painful reversal in the endless
cycle of loss and gain, and now
a new emptiness spreads out before her
and she doesn't know what to do.
But what kills me is when she tucks her hair

behind her ear and tries *not* to cry,
and fails, overcome by this sadness,
so that I feel it, too, a great swell lifts
and carries me and almost pulls me under—
and then I'm in the thick of it,
wishing her to be well, to be safe,
to be happy, as if my life
depended on it.

cold spring morning
close the window
or listen to the warbler?

not so different—
veined spring leaf
and my ancient hand

feet hurt, back hurts,
head hurts—
balanced at least!

coming unstitched
even the fake flowers
grow old

I put my glasses on
to see the fog
        more clearly

scattered crocuses
as if someone had planted
birdsong

the pain is still there
weeping willow
   my father cut down

regretting something I said
I turn the lampshade
to hide the seam

fifty years ago: seeds,
before that, nothing—
    oak trees outside my window

lost in a fantasy—
the framed kanji for compassion
falls to the floor

sleepless night
Buddha unbothered
on the altar

gently with an upturned broom
guiding the hummingbird
out the window

Non-harming

I wonder what the neighbors think when they see me
outside with the BB gun shooting at the pigeons
on our roof. I gave them a copy of my anthology,
The Poetry of Impermanence, Mindfulness, and Joy,
and the introduction makes me sound like
a person who probably wouldn't be shooting
at pigeons, even if only with a BB gun,
which doesn't really hurt them (I tell myself)
but simply encourages them to find
someplace else to deposit their smeary droppings
that threaten to turn one side of our house
into a bad Jackson Pollock painting.
"Honey, come look at this—isn't that
the mindfulness guy out there with a gun,
shooting at his own house?" I'm well aware
of the irony, but life's like that, isn't it?
A contradiction wrapped in an absurdity, etc.
Still, plunking pigeons with a BB gun
might not fall afoul of the injunction
to not cause harm. (I thought about shooting
myself in the foot just to see how much
it hurt but decided against it). I tried
placing scary-looking plastic owls strategically
around the roof but the pigeons laughed at that.

I tried an electronic device that sent out
a kind of sub-audible (to humans) shrieking,
imitative of a bird of prey, but they didn't fall for that
either. I always thought pigeons were dumb,
but now I'm not so sure. They've outsmarted me,
so far, not that that's any great accomplishment,
moving from one side of the roof to the other,
where the angle for firing is not so good,
and where the homeowner is exposed,
even in this early morning half-light,
to the watchful eyes of the neighbors.

Dudley Ball

In third grade only two kids got chased
around the playground.
One was a shaggy-haired boy,
I think his name was Peter,
who miraculously appeared in Lincoln,
Nebraska, from England, in 1963,
trailing clouds of Beatle-mania.
I watched in helpless amazement
as the girls squealed and took off
after him at every recess.
Hard to imagine what they would
have done had they caught him.
Held him down and kissed him?
Torn him limb from limb
like the maenads in Ovid?
The other was Dudley Ball, whose
yellowish face and bloodshot eyes
I now know indicated jaundice
and liver disease but at the time
signified only strangeness,
laughable ugliness, untouchable
difference from the rest of us.
The other boys chased him,
threw kickballs at him, thrilled

they could zing a ball at a weird kid
named Dudley Ball. "Hey Dudley,
have a ball!" "Dudley Ball, what a dud!"
The red hair and freckles, puffy cheeks
and constant perspiration, amplified
his otherness. No one spoke to him.
But why do I see his face so clearly now,
the fear and loneliness in his eyes?
The faces of all the others I've forgotten.
I was outraged at the injustice of it,
the cruelty of the schoolyard taunts.
I tried to intervene but couldn't
put the pack off his scent.
I told the teacher but can't recall
if she did anything about it.
And then he stopped coming to school.
A few months later, we were told he'd died.
I wish now I'd said a kind word
to him, tried harder to protect him.
I had my own strangenesses,
though mine were mostly invisible.
I wish I'd put my arm around his shoulder,
asked him to eat his lunch with me.
We could have watched together
the screeching girls, their mad pursuit,
and marveled at the vagaries of luck
and circumstance that exalt some

and cast down others, dealing out
adoration and ridicule in unequal measure.
We wouldn't have talked that way
back then, of course. More likely
we would have sat in awkward silence,
or talked about what we wanted
to be when we grew up.
Or maybe compared our cowlicks —
I remember now how alike ours were,
a cresting ocean wave
on the right side of our foreheads,
as though we'd each been licked
by the same thick-tongued cow,
a calm old cow who saw all our fears
and flaws and loved us
just the same.

Design

Strung be-
tween

rose
bushes

lit with
late

afternoon
light

this spider
web

pushed
and pulled

by the breeze
breathing

it seems
and knowing

just how
much to give

in either
direction

without
breaking—

an exemplary
figure

perfectly
designed

to catch
and hold

small
insects

this
sunlight

my fluttering
attention.

Bigleaf Maples

I like the way the roots of these bigleaf maple trees
muscle up through the ground like mountain ranges,
some of them with fern moss forests on their slopes.
I step over them like a god bestriding the earth.

But when I crane my neck to look up, I see I cannot see
their crowns, so high are they, and to them I must seem
a needlessly complicated creature, one who walks
and thinks and worries and sometimes stops to look.

And now the roots look like cresting waves or ripples
over creek rocks, and the path becomes a stream.
I'm walking upstream, seen by the unseen.

Something and Nothing

There's something to be said
for having nothing to say,

though I don't know what
that is, or isn't, just as

there's something to be
known about not-knowing,

which I would tell you
if I could. There must be

something to be gained
by losing, a seed of victory

buried in every failure,
else I would not be here.

Clearly, there's something
to be desired about being

beyond desire, as the sages
never tire of telling us,

and nothing more fulfilling
than emptying yourself out—

no ground beneath your feet,
nothing to hold onto, no handrail,

no belief, only this bright,
self-sustaining air, and a falling

that feels like floating.

No-Self

I tell myself
there is

no self—
I am just

a place
where the

universe
happens

to be
happening

telling itself
through me.

Passing Through

Nothing
sticks

to
space

everything
passes

right
through

leaving
and

leaving
no trace—

falling
stars and

flocks of
geese

a single
leaf

trains
of thought

and
real trains

threading
the

distance
their

mournful
honking in-

separable
from silence.

Above the Clackamas

I dip my mind
into the river

send my thoughts
downstream

in dissipating
swirls over

the temporary
eternity of rocks

I thought I
needed them

and sit between
two small fires

of Scotch broom
bushes on

the bank
each petal tipped

with slanted
light

and there is
stillness here—

flowing going
nowhere clean.

On Turning Sixty-Four

The slowing down
is speeding up.

.

Just This

Splash of
blood

red
quince

behind
the ash tree.

Morning, East Wallingford

Morning in East Wallingford,
not to be confused with
Wallingford proper,
down the road
a few miles
here in Vermont:
a bifurcated village.
Nothing much is
happening.
We had a thunderstorm
last night and now
bullfrogs are squawking
from the pond, as if
the storm had lodged
fragments of thunder
in their throats,
a wet and rubbery sound,
mildly insistent,
counterpointed by
faint birdsong
against a backdrop
of highway traffic,
cars and trucks,
the human contribution

to the soundscape.
The luna moth
we found last night
affixed to the porch railing
is gone, swept away by
the wind probably.
A fabulous creature,
green and leaflike,
with delicate orange ferns
for antennae and a curlicue
on each wing, added
for what purpose?
A mystery.
My wife is asleep upstairs,
her mother and father
a little further down the road.
I sit here feeling content,
even as I know the world
as we know it is ending,
happiness resting
in the pit of my stomach,
a calm excitement,
my mind free of anger,
resentment, ambition, regret.
Twelve raindrops hang
from the window sash,
gathering weight.

One or two look ready
to fall, but who
knows when
that will happen.
Pearled, light-filled,
each one a condensation
of cloud called downward
by invisible forces,
just as we are,
falling but not yet fallen,
held between earth
and sky, then and now,
and now the rain begins again.

Acknowledgments

I'm extremely grateful to the editors of the following journals for first publishing some of the poems collected here.

The American Journal of Poetry, Barrow Street, The Best American Poetry (1999, 2016), *Boulevard, Cloudbank, The Cortland Review, Frogpond, The Gettysburg Review, Kingfisher, Lion's Roar, The Manhattan Review, New Ohio Review, New South, NOON: journal of the short poem, Ploughshares, Plume, Poetry, Poetry Daily, Poetry Northwest, Presence, Prairie Schooner, Rattle, The Southern Review, The Southern Poetry Review, The Sun Magazine, Third Coast, This Land, Verse Daily, The Virginia Quarterly Review, The Westchester Review, The Writers Almanac.*

My thanks to Wisdom Publications for the use of poems published in *Dharma Talk* (2023) and to the University of Wisconsin Press for the use of poems published in *Sea of Faith* (2004), *Help Is on the Way* (2012), and *No Day at the Beach* (2020).

I'm deeply thankful to these friends and poets for their invaluable feedback on the poems collected here: Andrea Hollander, Fred Muratori, Heather Sellers, Justin Rigamonti, Chuck Moshontz, Ron Moshontz, and to my wife, Alice Boyd, who makes it all possible.

Profound thanks as well to Daniel Aitken, Brianna Quick, Patty McKenna, Ben Gleason, and the whole Wisdom team for bringing this book so beautifully to fruition and for continuing to support my work. Publishing with Wisdom has been a blessing beyond all dreams.

Notes

17 **"Poem About Nothing"**: The haiku included here—"long after / the call to prayer / the bell rope swaying"—is by Steve Sanfield from *No Other Business Here: A Haiku Correspondence*, coauthored by John Brandi. Used with the permission of the authors.

122 **"To Make the Wound More Beautiful"**: The novel referenced here is *Cutting for Stone* by Abraham Verghese.

131 **"To Make the Wound More Beautiful"**: The tanka included here is from *Awesome Nightfall: The Life, Times, and Poetry of Saigyō* by William R. LaFleur.

158 **"Signs and Wonderings"**: The book mentioned here is *When Breath Becomes Air* by Paul Kalanithi.

185 **"Dick's Kitchen Metaphysical"**: The book mentioned in the first line is *Knowledge of Higher Worlds and Its Attainment* by Rudolf Steiner.

210 **"Metta"**: The book referenced in the first line is *Loving-Kindness in Plain English: The Practice of Metta* by Bhante Gunaratana.

About the Author

 John Brehm is the author of four previous books of poetry: *Sea of Faith, Help Is on the Way, No Day at the Beach,* and *Dharma Talk.* He has published two anthologies, *The Poetry of Impermanence, Mindfulness, and Joy* and *The Poetry of Grief, Gratitude, and Reverence,* as well as a book of essays, *The Dharma of Poetry: How Poems Can Deepen Your Spiritual Practice and Open You to Joy.* He lives in Portland, Oregon, and can be found online at johnbrehmpoet.com.

Choose Your Next Inspiration

Wisdom Dharma Chat: John Brehm, October 2023

Please enjoy this lightly edited recording of our
Wisdom Dharma Chat with special guest, John
Brehm. During this *Wisdom Dharma Chat*, host
Daniel Aitken and John discuss John's process while
creating poetry, John reads some select poems from
his poetry volume *Dharma Talk*, and much more.
https://wisdomexperience.org/wisdom-dharma
-chat-john-brehm-october-2023/

Poetry of Impermanence, Mindfulness, and Joy

"This collection would make a lovely gift for a
poetry-loving or Dharma-practicing friend; it could
also serve as a wonderful gateway to either topic for
the uninitiated."—*Tricycle: The Buddhist Review*

Dharma Talk

Poems

"Think of this collection as a Guidebook to
Emptiness—to everything and nothing (which, as
the poet tells us, are interchangeable). Brehm gives
us a taste of that everything in images ranging from
jasmine blossoms placed beside the bed to perfume
the dreamer's sleep, to a brain bathed in sea salt and
lavender. These collected lines hang in the air like
the spider's web described in Brehm's poem 'Design':
'knowing / just how / much to give / in either /
direction / without breaking.' *Dharma Talk* is full
of wonders."—Danusha Laméris, author of *Bonfire
Opera*

The Poetry of Grief, Gratitude, and Reverence

"This beautiful and poignant poetry will reach
places in your mind and heart that you didn't
know existed."—Joanne Cacciatore, PhD, author
of *Bearing the Unbearable: Love, Loss, and the
Heartbreaking Path of Grief*

The Dharma of Poetry

How Poems Can Deepen Your Spiritual Practice and Open You to Joy

"*The Dharma of Poetry* is a warm invitation to explore the beauty of our own lives, retrieving a sense of wonder and mystery as we navigate both the immediate and the timeless. John Brehm has done a masterful job in reminding us of the power of our own poetic sensibilities."—Joseph Goldstein, author of *The Experience of Insight*, *A Heart Full of Peace*, and *Mindfulness: A Practical Guide to Awakening*

About Wisdom Publications

Wisdom Publications is the leading publisher of classic and contemporary Buddhist books and practical works on mindfulness. To learn more about us or to explore our other books, please visit our website at wisdom.org or contact us at the address below.

Wisdom Publications
132 Perry Street
New York, NY 10014 USA

We are a 501(c)(3) organization, and donations in support of our mission are tax deductible.

Wisdom Publications is affiliated with the Foundation for the Preservation of the Mahayana Tradition (FPMT).